This Trip Planner Belongs To:

_____

Copyright © 2019 Sinepure Books

TRAVEL *Bucket List*

PLACES I WANT TO VISIT:

THINGS I WANT TO SEE:

TOP 3 DESTINATIONS:

TRAVEL *Plans*

DESTINATION: **DATE:**

PLACES TO STAY

THINGS TO SEE

WHERE TO EAT

RECOMMENDATIONS

TRIP BUDGET *Planner*

DESTINATION:

AMOUNT NEEDED:

OUR GOAL DATE:

DEPOSIT TRACKER

AMOUNT DEPOSITED:　　　　　　　　**DATE DEPOSITED:**

TRIP BUDGET *Planner*

DESTINATION:

AMOUNT NEEDED:

OUR GOAL DATE:

DEPOSIT TRACKER

AMOUNT DEPOSITED: **DATE DEPOSITED:**

TRAVEL *Planner*
PRE-TRAVEL CHECKLIST

1 MONTH BEFORE

- [ ]
- [ ]
- [ ]
- [ ]
- [ ]

2 WEEKS BEFORE

- [ ]
- [ ]
- [ ]
- [ ]
- [ ]

1 WEEK BEFORE

- [ ]
- [ ]
- [ ]
- [ ]
- [ ]

2 DAYS BEFORE

- [ ]
- [ ]
- [ ]
- [ ]
- [ ]

24 HOURS BEFORE

- [ ]
- [ ]
- [ ]
- [ ]
- [ ]

DAY OF TRAVEL

- [ ]
- [ ]
- [ ]
- [ ]
- [ ]

PACKING *Check List*

DOCUMENTS

- [ ] PASSPORT
- [ ] DRIVER'S LICENSE
- [ ] VISA
- [ ] PLANE TICKETS
- [ ] LOCAL CURRENCY
- [ ] INSURANCE CARD
- [ ] HEALTH CARD
- [ ] OTHER ID
- [ ] HOTEL INFORMATION
- [ ] _____

CLOTHING

- [ ] UNDERWEAR / SOCKS
- [ ] SWIM WEAR
- [ ] T-SHIRTS
- [ ] JEANS/PANTS
- [ ] SHORTS
- [ ] SKIRTS / DRESSES
- [ ] JACKET / COAT
- [ ] SLEEPWEAR
- [ ] SHOES
- [ ] _____

PERSONAL ITEMS

- [ ] SHAMPOO
- [ ] RAZORS
- [ ] COSMETICS
- [ ] HAIR BRUSH
- [ ] LIP BALM
- [ ] WATER BOTTLE
- [ ] SOAP
- [ ] TOOTHBRUSH
- [ ] JEWELRY
- [ ] _____

ELECTRONICS

- [ ] CELL PHONE
- [ ] CHARGER
- [ ] LAPTOP
- [ ] BATTERIES
- [ ] EARPHONES
- [ ] FLASH DRIVE
- [ ] MEMORY CARD
- [ ] _____
- [ ] _____
- [ ] _____

HEALTH & SAFETY

- [ ] HAND SANITIZER
- [ ] SUNSCREEN
- [ ] VITAMIN SUPPLEMENTS
- [ ] BANDAIDS
- [ ] ADVIL/TYLENOL
- [ ] CONTACTS / GLASSES
- [ ] COLD/FLU MEDS
- [ ] _____
- [ ] _____
- [ ] _____

OTHER ESSENTIALS

- [ ] _____
- [ ] _____
- [ ] _____
- [ ] _____
- [ ] _____
- [ ] _____
- [ ] _____
- [ ] _____
- [ ] _____
- [ ] _____

PACKING *Check List*

DATE OF TRIP: _____   DURATION: _____

PACKING *Check List*

DATE OF TRIP: DURATION:

OUTFIT *Planner*

DAY: DESTINATION: PACKED: ☐

DAY: EVENING:

ACTIVITY:
OUTFIT:
SHOES:
ACC:

DAY: DESTINATION: PACKED: ☐

DAY: EVENING:

ACTIVITY:
OUTFIT:
SHOES:
ACC:

DAY: DESTINATION: PACKED: ☐

DAY: EVENING:

ACTIVITY:
OUTFIT:
SHOES:
ACC:

FLIGHT *Information*

DATE: DESTINATION:

AIRLINE:	
BOOKING NUMBER:	
DEPARTURE DATE:	
BOARDING TIME:	
GATE NUMBER:	
SEAT NUMBER:	
FLIGHT DURATION:	
ARRIVAL / LANDING TIME:	

DATE: DESTINATION:

AIRLINE:	
BOOKING NUMBER:	
DEPARTURE DATE:	
BOARDING TIME:	
GATE NUMBER:	
SEAT NUMBER:	
FLIGHT DURATION:	
ARRIVAL / LANDING TIME:	

FLIGHT *Information*

DATE: DESTINATION:

AIRLINE:	
BOOKING NUMBER:	
DEPARTURE DATE:	
BOARDING TIME:	
GATE NUMBER:	
SEAT NUMBER:	
FLIGHT DURATION:	
ARRIVAL / LANDING TIME:	

DATE: DESTINATION:

AIRLINE:	
BOOKING NUMBER:	
DEPARTURE DATE:	
BOARDING TIME:	
GATE NUMBER:	
SEAT NUMBER:	
FLIGHT DURATION:	
ARRIVAL / LANDING TIME:	

Hotel/Flight *Information*

HOTEL INFORMATION

NAME OF HOTEL:

ADDRESS:

PHONE NUMBER:

CONFIRMATION #:

RATE PER NIGHT:

FLIGHT INFORMATION

AIRLINE:

LOCATION:

FLIGHT #:

CHECK IN TIME:

DEPARTURE TIME:

REFERENCE #:

NOTES

Hotel/Flight *Information*

HOTEL INFORMATION

NAME OF HOTEL:

ADDRESS:

PHONE NUMBER:

CONFIRMATION #:

RATE PER NIGHT:

FLIGHT INFORMATION

AIRLINE:

LOCATION:

FLIGHT #:

CHECK IN TIME:

DEPARTURE TIME:

REFERENCE #:

NOTES

Car Rental/Event *Information*

CAR RENTAL INFORMATION

COMPANY:

ADDRESS:

PHONE NUMBER:

CONFIRMATION #:

TOTAL COST:

EVENT INFORMATION

EVENT NAME:

LOCATION:

PHONE NUMBER:

START TIME:

OTHER:

NOTES

Car Rental/Event *Information*

CAR RENTAL INFORMATION

COMPANY:

ADDRESS:

PHONE NUMBER:

CONFIRMATION #:

TOTAL COST:

EVENT INFORMATION

EVENT NAME:

LOCATION:

PHONE NUMBER:

START TIME:

OTHER:

NOTES

VACATION *Planner*
DAILY ITINERARY

DATE: _____

LOCATION: _____

BUDGET: _____

TOP ACTIVITIES

MEAL PLANNER

TIME: SCHEDULE:

EXPENSES

TOTAL COST: _____

NOTES:

VACATION *Planner*
DAILY ITINERARY

DATE: _____

LOCATION: _____

BUDGET: _____

TOP ACTIVITIES

MEAL PLANNER

TIME: SCHEDULE:

EXPENSES

TOTAL COST: _____

NOTES:

VACATION *Planner*
DAILY ITINERARY

DATE: _____

LOCATION: _____

BUDGET: _____

☀️ ⛅ 🌦️ ☁️ ⛈️

MEAL PLANNER

EXPENSES

TOTAL COST: _____

TOP ACTIVITIES

TIME: SCHEDULE:

NOTES:

VACATION *Planner*
DAILY ITINERARY

DATE: _____

LOCATION: _____

BUDGET: _____

TOP ACTIVITIES

MEAL PLANNER

TIME: SCHEDULE:

EXPENSES

TOTAL COST: _____

NOTES:

VACATION *Planner*
DAILY ITINERARY

DATE: _____

LOCATION: _____

BUDGET: _____

TOP ACTIVITIES

MEAL PLANNER

TIME: SCHEDULE:

EXPENSES

TOTAL COST: _____

NOTES:

VACATION *Planner*
DAILY ITINERARY

DATE: _____

LOCATION: _____

BUDGET: _____

TOP ACTIVITIES

MEAL PLANNER

TIME: SCHEDULE:

EXPENSES

TOTAL COST: _____

NOTES:

VACATION *Planner*
DAILY ITINERARY

DATE: _____

LOCATION: _____

BUDGET: _____

TOP ACTIVITIES

MEAL PLANNER

TIME: SCHEDULE:

EXPENSES

TOTAL COST: _____

NOTES:

VACATION *Planner*
DAILY ITINERARY

DATE: _____

LOCATION: _____

BUDGET: _____

TOP ACTIVITIES

MEAL PLANNER

TIME:		SCHEDULE:

EXPENSES

TOTAL COST: _____

NOTES:

VACATION *Planner*
DAILY ITINERARY

DATE: _____

LOCATION: _____

BUDGET: _____

☀️ ⛅ 🌦️ ☁️ ⛈️

TOP ACTIVITIES

MEAL PLANNER

TIME: SCHEDULE:

EXPENSES

TOTAL COST: _____

NOTES:

VACATION *Planner*
DAILY ITINERARY

DATE: _____

LOCATION: _____

BUDGET: _____

☀️ ⛅ 🌦️ ☁️ ⛈️

TOP ACTIVITIES

MEAL PLANNER

TIME: SCHEDULE:

EXPENSES

TOTAL COST: _____

NOTES:

VACATION *Planner*
DAILY ITINERARY

DATE: _____

LOCATION: _____

BUDGET: _____

TOP ACTIVITIES

MEAL PLANNER

TIME: SCHEDULE:

EXPENSES

TOTAL COST: _____

NOTES:

VACATION *Planner*
DAILY ITINERARY

DATE: _____

LOCATION: _____

BUDGET: _____

TOP ACTIVITIES

MEAL PLANNER

TIME: SCHEDULE:

EXPENSES

TOTAL COST: _____

NOTES:

VACATION *Planner*
DAILY ITINERARY

DATE: _____

LOCATION: _____

BUDGET: _____

TOP ACTIVITIES

MEAL PLANNER

TIME: SCHEDULE:

EXPENSES

TOTAL COST: _____

NOTES:

VACATION *Planner*
DAILY ITINERARY

DATE: _____

LOCATION: _____

BUDGET: _____

TOP ACTIVITIES

MEAL PLANNER

TIME: SCHEDULE:

EXPENSES

TOTAL COST: _____

NOTES:

DAILY TRAVEL *Planner*

MON

TUE

WED

THU

DAILY TRAVEL *Planner*

FRI

SAT

SUN

never STOP exploring

DAILY TRAVEL *Planner*

MON

TUE

WED

THU

DAILY TRAVEL *Planner*

FRI

SAT

SUN

never STOP exploring

TRAVEL EXPENSE *Tracker*

DESTINATION: BUDGET GOAL:

DATE:	DESCRIPTION:	CURRENCY:	AMOUNT:

TOTAL EXPENSES:

TRAVEL EXPENSE *Tracker*

DESTINATION: BUDGET GOAL:

DATE:	DESCRIPTION:	CURRENCY:	AMOUNT:
			TOTAL EXPENSES:

TRAVEL EXPENSE *Tracker*

DESTINATION: BUDGET GOAL:

DATE:	DESCRIPTION:	CURRENCY:	AMOUNT:

TOTAL EXPENSES:

TRAVEL EXPENSE *Tracker*

DESTINATION: BUDGET GOAL:

DATE:	DESCRIPTION:	CURRENCY:	AMOUNT:

TOTAL EXPENSES:

TRAVEL *Journal*

Bon Voyage

TRAVEL *Bucket List*

PLACES I WANT TO VISIT:

THINGS I WANT TO SEE:

TOP 3 DESTINATIONS:

TRAVEL *Plans*

DESTINATION:　　　　　　　　　　　**DATE:**

PLACES TO STAY

THINGS TO SEE

WHERE TO EAT

RECOMMENDATIONS

TRIP BUDGET *Planner*

DESTINATION:

AMOUNT NEEDED:

OUR GOAL DATE:

DEPOSIT TRACKER

AMOUNT DEPOSITED:　　　　　　　　**DATE DEPOSITED:**

TRIP BUDGET *Planner*

DESTINATION:

AMOUNT NEEDED:

OUR GOAL DATE:

DEPOSIT TRACKER

AMOUNT DEPOSITED:　　　　　　　　**DATE DEPOSITED:**

TRAVEL *Planner*
PRE-TRAVEL CHECKLIST

1 MONTH BEFORE

- [ ]
- [ ]
- [ ]
- [ ]
- [ ]

2 WEEKS BEFORE

- [ ]
- [ ]
- [ ]
- [ ]
- [ ]

1 WEEK BEFORE

- [ ]
- [ ]
- [ ]
- [ ]
- [ ]

2 DAYS BEFORE

- [ ]
- [ ]
- [ ]
- [ ]
- [ ]

24 HOURS BEFORE

- [ ]
- [ ]
- [ ]
- [ ]
- [ ]

DAY OF TRAVEL

- [ ]
- [ ]
- [ ]
- [ ]
- [ ]

PACKING *Check List*

DOCUMENTS

- [ ] PASSPORT
- [ ] DRIVER'S LICENSE
- [ ] VISA
- [ ] PLANE TICKETS
- [ ] LOCAL CURRENCY
- [ ] INSURANCE CARD
- [ ] HEALTH CARD
- [ ] OTHER ID
- [ ] HOTEL INFORMATION
- [ ] _____

CLOTHING

- [ ] UNDERWEAR / SOCKS
- [ ] SWIM WEAR
- [ ] T-SHIRTS
- [ ] JEANS/PANTS
- [ ] SHORTS
- [ ] SKIRTS / DRESSES
- [ ] JACKET / COAT
- [ ] SLEEPWEAR
- [ ] SHOES
- [ ] _____

PERSONAL ITEMS

- [ ] SHAMPOO
- [ ] RAZORS
- [ ] COSMETICS
- [ ] HAIR BRUSH
- [ ] LIP BALM
- [ ] WATER BOTTLE
- [ ] SOAP
- [ ] TOOTHBRUSH
- [ ] JEWELRY
- [ ] _____

ELECTRONICS

- [ ] CELL PHONE
- [ ] CHARGER
- [ ] LAPTOP
- [ ] BATTERIES
- [ ] EARPHONES
- [ ] FLASH DRIVE
- [ ] MEMORY CARD
- [ ] _____
- [ ] _____
- [ ] _____

HEALTH & SAFETY

- [ ] HAND SANITIZER
- [ ] SUNSCREEN
- [ ] VITAMIN SUPPLEMENTS
- [ ] BANDAIDS
- [ ] ADVIL/TYLENOL
- [ ] CONTACTS / GLASSES
- [ ] COLD/FLU MEDS
- [ ] _____
- [ ] _____
- [ ] _____

OTHER ESSENTIALS

- [ ] _____
- [ ] _____
- [ ] _____
- [ ] _____
- [ ] _____
- [ ] _____
- [ ] _____
- [ ] _____
- [ ] _____
- [ ] _____

PACKING *Check List*

DATE OF TRIP: DURATION:

PACKING *Check List*

DATE OF TRIP: DURATION:

OUTFIT *Planner*

DAY: DESTINATION: PACKED: ☐

DAY: EVENING:

ACTIVITY:
OUTFIT:
SHOES:
ACC:

DAY: DESTINATION: PACKED: ☐

DAY: EVENING:

ACTIVITY:
OUTFIT:
SHOES:
ACC:

DAY: DESTINATION: PACKED: ☐

DAY: EVENING:

ACTIVITY:
OUTFIT:
SHOES:
ACC:

FLIGHT *Information*

DATE: DESTINATION:

AIRLINE:	
BOOKING NUMBER:	
DEPARTURE DATE:	
BOARDING TIME:	
GATE NUMBER:	
SEAT NUMBER:	
FLIGHT DURATION:	
ARRIVAL / LANDING TIME:	

DATE: DESTINATION:

AIRLINE:	
BOOKING NUMBER:	
DEPARTURE DATE:	
BOARDING TIME:	
GATE NUMBER:	
SEAT NUMBER:	
FLIGHT DURATION:	
ARRIVAL / LANDING TIME:	

FLIGHT *Information*

DATE: DESTINATION:

AIRLINE:	
BOOKING NUMBER:	
DEPARTURE DATE:	
BOARDING TIME:	
GATE NUMBER:	
SEAT NUMBER:	
FLIGHT DURATION:	
ARRIVAL / LANDING TIME:	

DATE: DESTINATION:

AIRLINE:	
BOOKING NUMBER:	
DEPARTURE DATE:	
BOARDING TIME:	
GATE NUMBER:	
SEAT NUMBER:	
FLIGHT DURATION:	
ARRIVAL / LANDING TIME:	

Hotel/Flight *Information*

HOTEL INFORMATION

NAME OF HOTEL:

ADDRESS:

PHONE NUMBER:

CONFIRMATION #:

RATE PER NIGHT:

FLIGHT INFORMATION

AIRLINE:

LOCATION:

FLIGHT #:

CHECK IN TIME:

DEPARTURE TIME:

REFERENCE #:

NOTES

Hotel/Flight Information

HOTEL INFORMATION

NAME OF HOTEL:

ADDRESS:

PHONE NUMBER:

CONFIRMATION #:

RATE PER NIGHT:

FLIGHT INFORMATION

AIRLINE:

LOCATION:

FLIGHT #:

CHECK IN TIME:

DEPARTURE TIME:

REFERENCE #:

NOTES

Car Rental/Event *Information*

CAR RENTAL INFORMATION

COMPANY:

ADDRESS:

PHONE NUMBER:

CONFIRMATION #:

TOTAL COST:

EVENT INFORMATION

EVENT NAME:

LOCATION:

PHONE NUMBER:

START TIME:

OTHER:

NOTES

Car Rental/Event *Information*

CAR RENTAL INFORMATION

COMPANY:

ADDRESS:

PHONE NUMBER:

CONFIRMATION #:

TOTAL COST:

EVENT INFORMATION

EVENT NAME:

LOCATION:

PHONE NUMBER:

START TIME:

OTHER:

NOTES

VACATION *Planner*
DAILY ITINERARY

DATE: _____

LOCATION: _____

BUDGET: _____

MEAL PLANNER

EXPENSES

TOTAL COST: _____

TOP ACTIVITIES

TIME: SCHEDULE:

NOTES:

VACATION *Planner*
DAILY ITINERARY

DATE: _____

LOCATION: _____

BUDGET: _____

TOP ACTIVITIES

MEAL PLANNER

TIME: SCHEDULE:

EXPENSES

TOTAL COST: _____

NOTES:

VACATION *Planner*
DAILY ITINERARY

DATE: _____

LOCATION: _____

BUDGET: _____

☀️ 🌤️ 🌦️ ☁️ ⛈️

MEAL PLANNER

EXPENSES

TOTAL COST: _____

TOP ACTIVITIES

TIME: SCHEDULE:

NOTES:

VACATION *Planner*
DAILY ITINERARY

DATE: _____

LOCATION: _____

BUDGET: _____

☀️ ⛅ 🌦️ ☁️ ⛈️

TOP ACTIVITIES

MEAL PLANNER

TIME: **SCHEDULE:**

EXPENSES

TOTAL COST: _____

NOTES:

VACATION *Planner*
DAILY ITINERARY

DATE: _____

LOCATION: _____

BUDGET: _____

☀️ ⛅ 🌦️ ☁️ ⛈️

TOP ACTIVITIES

MEAL PLANNER

TIME: SCHEDULE:

EXPENSES

TOTAL COST: _____

NOTES:

VACATION *Planner*
DAILY ITINERARY

DATE: _____

LOCATION: _____

BUDGET: _____

☀️ ⛅ 🌦️ ☁️ ⛈️

MEAL PLANNER

EXPENSES

TOTAL COST: _____

TOP ACTIVITIES

TIME: SCHEDULE:

NOTES:

VACATION *Planner*
DAILY ITINERARY

DATE: _____

LOCATION: _____

BUDGET: _____

TOP ACTIVITIES

MEAL PLANNER

TIME: SCHEDULE:

EXPENSES

TOTAL COST: _____

NOTES:

VACATION *Planner*
DAILY ITINERARY

DATE: _____

LOCATION: _____

BUDGET: _____

TOP ACTIVITIES

MEAL PLANNER

TIME: SCHEDULE:

EXPENSES

TOTAL COST: _____

NOTES:

VACATION *Planner*
DAILY ITINERARY

DATE: _____

LOCATION: _____

BUDGET: _____

☀️ 🌤️ 🌦️ ☁️ ⛈️

MEAL PLANNER

EXPENSES

TOTAL COST: _____

TOP ACTIVITIES

TIME: SCHEDULE:

NOTES:

VACATION *Planner*
DAILY ITINERARY

DATE: _____

LOCATION: _____

BUDGET: _____

TOP ACTIVITIES

MEAL PLANNER

TIME: SCHEDULE:

EXPENSES

TOTAL COST: _____

NOTES:

VACATION *Planner*
DAILY ITINERARY

DATE: _____
LOCATION: _____
BUDGET: _____

☀ ⛅ 🌦 ☁ ⛈

MEAL PLANNER

EXPENSES

TOTAL COST: _____

TOP ACTIVITIES

TIME: SCHEDULE:

NOTES:

VACATION *Planner*
DAILY ITINERARY

DATE: _____

LOCATION: _____

BUDGET: _____

TOP ACTIVITIES

MEAL PLANNER

TIME: SCHEDULE:

EXPENSES

TOTAL COST: _____

NOTES:

VACATION *Planner*
DAILY ITINERARY

DATE: _____

LOCATION: _____

BUDGET: _____

TOP ACTIVITIES

MEAL PLANNER

TIME: SCHEDULE:

EXPENSES

TOTAL COST: _____

NOTES:

VACATION *Planner*
DAILY ITINERARY

DATE: _____
LOCATION: _____
BUDGET: _____

☀️ ⛅ 🌦️ ☁️ ⛈️

MEAL PLANNER

EXPENSES

TOTAL COST: _____

TOP ACTIVITIES

TIME: SCHEDULE:

NOTES:

DAILY TRAVEL *Planner*

MON

TUE

WED

THU

DAILY TRAVEL *Planner*

FRI

SAT

SUN

never STOP exploring

DAILY TRAVEL *Planner*

MON

TUE

WED

THU

DAILY TRAVEL *Planner*

FRI

SAT

SUN

never STOP exploring

TRAVEL EXPENSE *Tracker*

DESTINATION: _____   BUDGET GOAL: _____

DATE:	DESCRIPTION:	CURRENCY:	AMOUNT:
		TOTAL EXPENSES:	

TRAVEL EXPENSE *Tracker*

DESTINATION: BUDGET GOAL:

DATE:	DESCRIPTION:	CURRENCY:	AMOUNT:
		TOTAL EXPENSES:	

TRAVEL EXPENSE *Tracker*

DESTINATION: BUDGET GOAL:

DATE:	DESCRIPTION:	CURRENCY:	AMOUNT:

TOTAL EXPENSES:

TRAVEL EXPENSE *Tracker*

DESTINATION: BUDGET GOAL:

DATE:	DESCRIPTION:	CURRENCY:	AMOUNT:
		TOTAL EXPENSES:	

TRAVEL *Journal*

Bon Voyage

TRAVEL *Bucket List*

PLACES I WANT TO VISIT:

THINGS I WANT TO SEE:

TOP 3 DESTINATIONS:

TRAVEL *Plans*

DESTINATION: DATE:

PLACES TO STAY

THINGS TO SEE

WHERE TO EAT

RECOMMENDATIONS

TRIP BUDGET *Planner*

DESTINATION:

AMOUNT NEEDED:

OUR GOAL DATE:

DEPOSIT TRACKER

AMOUNT DEPOSITED: **DATE DEPOSITED:**

TRIP BUDGET *Planner*

DESTINATION:

AMOUNT NEEDED:

OUR GOAL DATE:

DEPOSIT TRACKER

AMOUNT DEPOSITED: **DATE DEPOSITED:**

TRAVEL *Planner*
PRE-TRAVEL CHECKLIST

1 MONTH BEFORE

- [ ]
- [ ]
- [ ]
- [ ]
- [ ]

2 WEEKS BEFORE

- [ ]
- [ ]
- [ ]
- [ ]
- [ ]

1 WEEK BEFORE

- [ ]
- [ ]
- [ ]
- [ ]
- [ ]

2 DAYS BEFORE

- [ ]
- [ ]
- [ ]
- [ ]
- [ ]

24 HOURS BEFORE

- [ ]
- [ ]
- [ ]
- [ ]
- [ ]

DAY OF TRAVEL

- [ ]
- [ ]
- [ ]
- [ ]
- [ ]

PACKING Check List

DOCUMENTS

- ☐ PASSPORT
- ☐ DRIVER'S LICENSE
- ☐ VISA
- ☐ PLANE TICKETS
- ☐ LOCAL CURRENCY
- ☐ INSURANCE CARD
- ☐ HEALTH CARD
- ☐ OTHER ID
- ☐ HOTEL INFORMATION
- ☐ _____

CLOTHING

- ☐ UNDERWEAR / SOCKS
- ☐ SWIM WEAR
- ☐ T-SHIRTS
- ☐ JEANS/PANTS
- ☐ SHORTS
- ☐ SKIRTS / DRESSES
- ☐ JACKET / COAT
- ☐ SLEEPWEAR
- ☐ SHOES
- ☐ _____

PERSONAL ITEMS

- ☐ SHAMPOO
- ☐ RAZORS
- ☐ COSMETICS
- ☐ HAIR BRUSH
- ☐ LIP BALM
- ☐ WATER BOTTLE
- ☐ SOAP
- ☐ TOOTHBRUSH
- ☐ JEWELRY
- ☐ _____

ELECTRONICS

- ☐ CELL PHONE
- ☐ CHARGER
- ☐ LAPTOP
- ☐ BATTERIES
- ☐ EARPHONES
- ☐ FLASH DRIVE
- ☐ MEMORY CARD
- ☐ _____
- ☐ _____
- ☐ _____

HEALTH & SAFETY

- ☐ HAND SANITIZER
- ☐ SUNSCREEN
- ☐ VITAMIN SUPPLEMENTS
- ☐ BANDAIDS
- ☐ ADVIL/TYLENOL
- ☐ CONTACTS / GLASSES
- ☐ COLD/FLU MEDS
- ☐ _____
- ☐ _____
- ☐ _____

OTHER ESSENTIALS

- ☐ _____
- ☐ _____
- ☐ _____
- ☐ _____
- ☐ _____
- ☐ _____
- ☐ _____
- ☐ _____
- ☐ _____
- ☐ _____

PACKING *Check List*

DATE OF TRIP: DURATION:

PACKING *Check List*

DATE OF TRIP: DURATION:

OUTFIT *Planner*

DAY: DESTINATION: PACKED: ☐

DAY: EVENING:

ACTIVITY:
OUTFIT:
SHOES:
ACC:

DAY: DESTINATION: PACKED: ☐

DAY: EVENING:

ACTIVITY:
OUTFIT:
SHOES:
ACC:

DAY: DESTINATION: PACKED: ☐

DAY: EVENING:

ACTIVITY:
OUTFIT:
SHOES:
ACC:

FLIGHT *Information*

DATE: DESTINATION:

AIRLINE:	
BOOKING NUMBER:	
DEPARTURE DATE:	
BOARDING TIME:	
GATE NUMBER:	
SEAT NUMBER:	
FLIGHT DURATION:	
ARRIVAL / LANDING TIME:	

DATE: DESTINATION:

AIRLINE:	
BOOKING NUMBER:	
DEPARTURE DATE:	
BOARDING TIME:	
GATE NUMBER:	
SEAT NUMBER:	
FLIGHT DURATION:	
ARRIVAL / LANDING TIME:	

FLIGHT *Information*

DATE: _____   DESTINATION: _____

AIRLINE:	
BOOKING NUMBER:	
DEPARTURE DATE:	
BOARDING TIME:	
GATE NUMBER:	
SEAT NUMBER:	
FLIGHT DURATION:	
ARRIVAL / LANDING TIME:	

DATE: _____   DESTINATION: _____

AIRLINE:	
BOOKING NUMBER:	
DEPARTURE DATE:	
BOARDING TIME:	
GATE NUMBER:	
SEAT NUMBER:	
FLIGHT DURATION:	
ARRIVAL / LANDING TIME:	

Hotel/Flight *Information*

HOTEL INFORMATION

NAME OF HOTEL:

ADDRESS:

PHONE NUMBER:

CONFIRMATION #:

RATE PER NIGHT:

FLIGHT INFORMATION

AIRLINE:

LOCATION:

FLIGHT #:

CHECK IN TIME:

DEPARTURE TIME:

REFERENCE #:

NOTES

Hotel/Flight *Information*

HOTEL INFORMATION

NAME OF HOTEL:

ADDRESS:

PHONE NUMBER:

CONFIRMATION #:

RATE PER NIGHT:

FLIGHT INFORMATION

AIRLINE:

LOCATION:

FLIGHT #:

CHECK IN TIME:

DEPARTURE TIME:

REFERENCE #:

NOTES

Car Rental/Event *Information*

CAR RENTAL INFORMATION

COMPANY:

ADDRESS:

PHONE NUMBER:

CONFIRMATION #:

TOTAL COST:

EVENT INFORMATION

EVENT NAME:

LOCATION:

PHONE NUMBER:

START TIME:

OTHER:

NOTES

Car Rental/Event Information

CAR RENTAL INFORMATION

COMPANY:

ADDRESS:

PHONE NUMBER:

CONFIRMATION #:

TOTAL COST:

EVENT INFORMATION

EVENT NAME:

LOCATION:

PHONE NUMBER:

START TIME:

OTHER:

NOTES

VACATION *Planner*
DAILY ITINERARY

DATE: _____

LOCATION: _____

BUDGET: _____

TOP ACTIVITIES

MEAL PLANNER

TIME: SCHEDULE:

EXPENSES

TOTAL COST: _____

NOTES:

VACATION *Planner*
DAILY ITINERARY

DATE: _____

LOCATION: _____

BUDGET: _____

TOP ACTIVITIES

MEAL PLANNER

TIME: SCHEDULE:

EXPENSES

TOTAL COST: _____

NOTES:

VACATION *Planner*
DAILY ITINERARY

DATE: _____

LOCATION: _____

BUDGET: _____

TOP ACTIVITIES

MEAL PLANNER

TIME: SCHEDULE:

EXPENSES

TOTAL COST: _____

NOTES:

VACATION *Planner*
DAILY ITINERARY

DATE: _____

LOCATION: _____

BUDGET: _____

TOP ACTIVITIES

MEAL PLANNER

TIME: SCHEDULE:

EXPENSES

TOTAL COST: _____

NOTES:

VACATION *Planner*
DAILY ITINERARY

DATE: _____

LOCATION: _____

BUDGET: _____

TOP ACTIVITIES

MEAL PLANNER

TIME: SCHEDULE:

EXPENSES

TOTAL COST: _____

NOTES:

VACATION *Planner*
DAILY ITINERARY

DATE: _____

LOCATION: _____

BUDGET: _____

TOP ACTIVITIES

MEAL PLANNER

TIME: SCHEDULE:

EXPENSES

TOTAL COST: _____

NOTES:

VACATION *Planner*
DAILY ITINERARY

DATE: _____

LOCATION: _____

BUDGET: _____

TOP ACTIVITIES

MEAL PLANNER

TIME: SCHEDULE:

EXPENSES

TOTAL COST: _____

NOTES:

VACATION *Planner*
DAILY ITINERARY

DATE: _____

LOCATION: _____

BUDGET: _____

☀️ ⛅ 🌦️ ☁️ ⛈️

MEAL PLANNER

EXPENSES

TOTAL COST: _____

TOP ACTIVITIES

TIME: SCHEDULE:

NOTES:

VACATION *Planner*
DAILY ITINERARY

DATE: _____

LOCATION: _____

BUDGET: _____

TOP ACTIVITIES

MEAL PLANNER

TIME: SCHEDULE:

EXPENSES

TOTAL COST: _____

NOTES:

VACATION *Planner*
DAILY ITINERARY

DATE: _____

LOCATION: _____

BUDGET: _____

TOP ACTIVITIES

MEAL PLANNER

TIME: SCHEDULE:

EXPENSES

TOTAL COST: _____

NOTES:

VACATION *Planner*
DAILY ITINERARY

DATE: _____

LOCATION: _____

BUDGET: _____

☀️ ⛅ 🌦️ ☁️ ⛈️

TOP ACTIVITIES

MEAL PLANNER

TIME: SCHEDULE:

EXPENSES

TOTAL COST: _____

NOTES:

VACATION *Planner*
DAILY ITINERARY

DATE: _____

LOCATION: _____

BUDGET: _____

TOP ACTIVITIES

MEAL PLANNER

TIME: SCHEDULE:

EXPENSES

TOTAL COST: _____

NOTES:

VACATION *Planner*
DAILY ITINERARY

DATE: _____

LOCATION: _____

BUDGET: _____

☀️ 🌤️ 🌦️ ☁️ ⛈️

TOP ACTIVITIES

MEAL PLANNER

TIME: SCHEDULE:

EXPENSES

TOTAL COST: _____

NOTES:

VACATION *Planner*
DAILY ITINERARY

DATE: _____

LOCATION: _____

BUDGET: _____

TOP ACTIVITIES

MEAL PLANNER

TIME: SCHEDULE:

EXPENSES

TOTAL COST: _____

NOTES:

DAILY TRAVEL *Planner*

MON

TUE

WED

THU

DAILY TRAVEL *Planner*

FRI

SAT

SUN

never STOP exploring

DAILY TRAVEL *Planner*

MON

TUE

WED

THU

DAILY TRAVEL *Planner*

FRI

SAT

SUN

never STOP exploring

TRAVEL EXPENSE *Tracker*

DESTINATION:　　　　　　　　　BUDGET GOAL:

DATE:	DESCRIPTION:	CURRENCY:	AMOUNT:
			TOTAL EXPENSES:

TRAVEL EXPENSE *Tracker*

DESTINATION: BUDGET GOAL:

DATE:	DESCRIPTION:	CURRENCY:	AMOUNT:

TOTAL EXPENSES:

TRAVEL EXPENSE *Tracker*

DESTINATION: BUDGET GOAL:

DATE:	DESCRIPTION:	CURRENCY:	AMOUNT:

TOTAL EXPENSES:

TRAVEL EXPENSE *Tracker*

DESTINATION: BUDGET GOAL:

DATE:	DESCRIPTION:	CURRENCY:	AMOUNT:
		TOTAL EXPENSES:	

TRAVEL *Journal*

Bon Voyage

Made in the USA
Coppell, TX
17 March 2022